Our Story:
Martha & Pinkas Isaak

REVISED EDITION

The glory of children is their parents.
Proverbs 17:6

© 2020 Beth Gerson, M. David Isaak
Published by GERISA INC. All Rights Reserved
https://www.gerisabooks.org

Our Story: Martha & Pinkas Isaak — Rev. ed.

No part of this publication may be reproduced, stored in a retrieval system or transmitted in any form or by any means, electronic, mechanical, photocopying, recording, or otherwise without written permission of the editors.

Although every precaution has been taken to verify the accuracy of the information contained herein, the editors and publisher assume no responsibility for any errors or omissions. No liability is assumed for damages that may result from the use of information contained within.

ISBN: 978-1-7353296-2-8
Library of Congress Control Number: 2020918569

Includes bibliographical and historical references
Printed in the United States of America
First Edition 2011
Revised Edition 2020

Book design by Beth Gerson and M. David Isaak.

Cover photograph in the collection of
The Museum of Jewish Heritage–A Living Memorial to the Holocaust New York, NY.
Gift of Beth Gerson and M. David Isaak.

Our Story:
Martha & Pinkas Isaak

REVISED EDITION

Beth Gerson and M. David Isaak
EDITORS

OUR STORY: MARTHA & PINKAS ISAAK

TABLE OF CONTENTS

— • —

Acknowledgments   7

Introduction   9

CHAPTER ONE
    Leipzig   11

CHAPTER TWO
    Nuremberg to Berlin   21

CHAPTER THREE
    Berlin – And So We Met   29

CHAPTER FOUR
    Venice   41

CHAPTER 5
    London   45

CHAPTER SIX
    Llanelli, Wales   53

CHAPTER SEVEN
    Back in Wartime London   57

CHAPTER EIGHT
    Israel   67

CHAPTER NINE
    New York   79

Afterword   91

— • —

OUR STORY: MARTHA & PINKAS ISAAK

Acknowledgments

Martha and Pinkas Isaak fled Germany on December 4, 1938, three months after their wedding and nine months before Hitler invaded Poland. From the beginning, their 70 years as a couple were devoted to family and survival.

Forty pages of notes painstakingly written on yellow legal pads provided the essence of *Our Story: Martha & Pinkas Isaak*. This is Martha and Pinkas' story, conveyed in their words decades after the Holocaust. Care has been taken to ensure authenticity of voice, tone and message. Brief explanations provided in footnotes pertaining to historical events and the fate of family members are expanded in a companion publication entitled *Missing Pieces: A Family Story Retold*, (Isaak & Gerson, 2020).

Resources consulted in the process of clarifying historical details include the *Memorial Book of Victims of the Persecution of Jews Under the National Socialist Tyranny in Germany 1933-1945* in the German Federal Archives (*Das Bundesarchiv*), the Central Data Base of Shoah Victims' Names at Yad Vashem, the United States Holocaust Memorial Museum, the Museum of Jewish Heritage – A Living Memorial to the Holocaust, and JewishGen – Preserving Our History for Future Generations.

Martha and Pinkas knew well the pain of loss and the challenge of rebuilding. They left us with a legacy of faith, resilience, tradition, and hope for a better tomorrow.

New York, New York
December 2020

OUR STORY: MARTHA & PINKAS ISAAK

Introduction

What follows is a sincere attempt to present our story, individually since childhood and together as a couple through our 65th wedding anniversary, all in the context of the times during which the events described took place. Naturally, the recollection of events that happened in the past is subject to the inevitable risk of error. This is particularly true of our story. We never kept a diary, all of our photographs were lost during our move to Israel nearly 60 years ago, and, especially during the early years of our married life, events occurred at such a hectic pace that their chronology might sometimes be confused.

When our son Moish was married to Beth, he chose a quotation from the Talmud as his guiding light and had it printed on the wedding invitations he and Beth sent out. This is a free translation: "A couple that lives in harmony will feel blessed as if there was a heavenly presence residing over them." In our married life, Martha and I have often felt as if the hand of G-d was guiding and protecting us. We too felt the heavenly presence.

Let me indulge in a bit of number crunching. At the time I am writing this, I am 87 years old and Martha is 83. If you add these numbers up, you get $8 + 7 = 15$ and $8 + 3 = 11$; $15 + 11$ total 26, which is the numerical value of the Hebrew letters *Jud*, *Keh*, *Vav*, *Keh* – one of the names by which G-d is known. Throughout this narrative, you will read about times where this feeling of heavenly presence was, for us, very strong. Surely, it was this Divine Oversight that must have saved us from the pitfalls and disasters that could have been. We thank the good Lord for 65 years of harmonious togetherness and will be grateful for however many more years he will grant us.

Pinkas Isaak
Sunny Isles Beach, Florida
2004

Pinkas Isaak, 1936

Photograph in the editors' private collection

CHAPTER ONE
Leipzig

Pinkas narrates:

I was born on July 5, 1916. Actually, there was a discrepancy between my birth certificate, inscribed with the above date, and my vaccination certificate that lists my date of birth as July 7th. In order to avoid complications later on, I decided to take the 5th as my date of birth, but it is quite possible that I am actually two days younger than I claim to be.

My father, Alter Meier Isaak, was born in Tarnow. My mother, Mindl, whose maiden name was Ehrenreich, was born in Dukla. Both of these towns were in Galicia and later became part of southeastern Poland. My parents moved to Germany and settled in Ludwigshafen am Rhein.

I am the seventh of eight children. While my parents lived in Ludwigshafen, their first child was stillborn, followed by my oldest brother Elias Jacob, my sisters Fannie and Sali (Sascha), and my brother Bernhard, who was born in 1908. That same year, my parents moved to Leipzig, where my sister Hulda (who at her husband's request came to be known as Hilda), my brother Simon Jonas, my youngest brother Josef, and I were born. Today I am the only one surviving.

I have little knowledge about my grandparents apart from their names. My paternal grandfather's name was Moshe Dovid. My maternal grandfather was called Dov.

As far as I know, my father was orphaned at a young age. As an adult, he established a wholesale business that supplied linens and textiles to the itinerant peddlers who traveled around with baskets strapped to their backs, selling their merchandise to the farmers and townspeople in the surrounding villages. His sister was one of those peddlers. For her own reasons, she would not patronize her brother's business but every morning made a point of passing our house to shop at a competitor's store. This situation did not promote a close family relationship. Although we had little contact with my aunt, my sister Hilda was friendly with her two daughters.

My mother had a brother named Chaim. He and his wife Lotte lived in Lisbon with their children, a son and two daughters. Whenever Uncle Chaim came to Leipzig on one of his frequent business trips, he stayed with us.

During my early years, my father's business was quite successful. At that time he was considered "middle class rich." However, by the time I had finished elementary school, the steadily worsening conditions in Germany had caused my father's business to slow precipitously. In retrospect, I doubt whether it was producing enough income to cover our expenses.

I went to a public school, the 32nd *Volk Schule* (People's School), which was tuition free. For gifted children, they offered the opportunity to study a foreign language. I participated in that program, where I chose to study English. My brothers, Simon Jonas and Josef, and I spent our afternoons attending *Talmud Torah* (after school Hebrew program). One day, Rabbi Ephraim Carlebach, who headed the city's Jewish high school, came to examine the children and was astounded to find that the top students in three classes were named Isaak, but none of us was enrolled in his school. He contacted our parents and arranged for scholarships that enabled us to transfer from the public school to the Jewish high school.

At home, all of the children's needs were taken care of, but the warmth needed to support a happy family life was missing. Perhaps my father did not know how to display affection for his children because he was orphaned as a young boy. My mother was overworked and did not have the strength to cope. In addition to taking care of her large family, she had to make regular visits to some of my father's customers.

I do not remember having been given a toy as a child. The only plaything I remember is a game called "patchek." I whittled a block of wood into the shape of a cigar with a point on each end. I would hit the wooden "cigar" on one end with a small paddle, and, when it jumped in the air, I hit it again. The goal was to send it flying as far as possible.

My bar mitzvah was a very simple affair. My mother was away for a cure in Czechoslovakia to alleviate her constant pain and could not interrupt the treatment. All I did was chant four sentences of the *maftir* (the end of the weekly Torah portion), and my father provided a small *kiddush* (celebration meal) in *shul* (synagogue). My sister Sali, who wanted to bring some culture into my life, gave me a violin as a bar mitzvah present. Four weeks later, I put an ad in a local newspaper stating, "Violin for sale. Bicycle wanted." Since then, I've known how to ride a bicycle.

I did have some outside activities. I joined a group that met once a week to go jogging in the Rosenthal City Park. In addition, I became a member of the Bar Kochba Sports Club. The club met once a week at an indoor swimming pool. Since I couldn't afford to pay the extra cost of swimming lessons, I was only able to do the "dog paddle." This gave me enough courage to go to an outdoor pool the next summer and dive headfirst from a 10-meter diving board. Believe it or not, I even joined their boxing club, though I never climbed into a ring. My participation was limited to skipping rope and using the punching bag.

In addition to school and participating in recreational activities, I earned pocket money by tutoring and giving bar mitzvah lessons. I also sang as a soprano soloist in a choir for Cantor Stern, for which I received a small monthly payment.

I managed to complete high school after eight years of education at the Ephraim Carlebach School. The classes were co-ed and, to my chagrin, the top student in my class was a girl. I maintained a 2-A average on a scale of 1-5. A most embarrassing moment occurred at the final graduation ceremony. After all the speeches, the graduating students were handed blue folders containing their certificates. When I peeked inside my folder, I found a note advising me that I could pick up my certificate at the school office after making payment for two months of tuition in arrears.

The year was 1934, and there was no earthly chance of continuing a meaningful higher education. Here I must note that, after the defeat of Nazi Germany, the new government started a program of *Wiedergutmachung*, translated as "Making Good Again" or restitution. Under this program, I, along with thousands of other Jews, was awarded a one-time payment of $1,000 as compensation for having been deprived of a higher education.

When I started to look for employment, I found that, like the halls of academia, entry into the labor market was seriously restricted and often denied to Jews. I finally found an entry level job with a furrier by the name of Becker.

Mr. Becker imported raw pelts from Holland, which he cleaned up and treated for use as soft fur in cheap garments. He specialized in handling civet cats. These cats had beautiful, fawn colored striped coats, like a tiger. Unfortunately, the pelts did not look that way when they arrived. After the animals were killed and skinned, they were bundled and shipped with the skin outside and the fur inside. The first step in the process of readying the fur for use in garments consisted of pulling the fur to the outside.

My job for eight hours every workday was to reach in and do whatever was needed to bring the fur outside. I lasted at that job for about two weeks. For those two weeks I was in hell. I had constant nausea, was sick, and could not sleep. Although my boss assured me that I would advance to the "next stage," I quit this job. The experience left me with an aversion to cats and small dogs.

Thinking back to my youth, I recognize that, as conditions in Germany worsened, our home life became increasingly difficult. What held the family together was the love we shared for our mother. Her life was not easy, even before she was married. As a girl, she made money by helping neighbors make noodles for *Shabbos* (Sabbath). This was not an easy task. It involved kneading the dough, rolling it flat, and cutting it into thin strips. In those days, there was no ready-made pasta available.

In retrospect, I feel that we all resented the fact that our mother had to call regularly on customers who lived in the surrounding villages, while my father stayed at home. She took care of our family of ten in the evening and early in the day on Monday and Tuesday. As she grew older, she had to go at least once a year to Marienbad for rest and recuperation. While my mother was away, my sisters, Sali and Hilda, took care of the housekeeping duties.

On May 10, 1933, my dear mother succumbed and passed away at a relatively young age, at the Jewish Eitingon Hospital. I do not remember the cause of her death. What I do remember most vividly is that, when I saw her on her deathbed, her *sheitel* (wig) had been removed and her hair underneath was snow white. Never before had I seen her without her wig. I had just assumed that the natural color of her hair was dark brown.

I have a vivid memory of the day my mother died. Across the street from the hospital, there was a fairground with a carousel, rides, music, swings, and happy children. Leaving the hospital, I felt full of rage. Here a human being, my mother, had passed away, and the whole world ignored it. People were laughing, playing music, and having a good time.

With my mother's death, the family began drifting apart. For a while, my sister Hilda did her best to keep the family going, but she found it very difficult. I remember one incident when Hilda prepared meat for the *Shabbos* table and was not sure whether she had followed the rules for koshering. After salting the meat, she did not remember whether she had soaked it long enough before putting it into the pot.

She went to the Rabbi to ask a *shaaleh* (religious question). After asking Hilda about the size of the family and the availability of other meat, he told her it was kosher. My sister, seeing an opening to ease her work, said, "In other words, it is not so critical how long you soak the meat." The Rabbi wagged his finger at Hilda and said, "Go home, child. But the next time you come to ask me, it will be *treif* (forbidden, not kosher)."

It was around this time that my oldest brother Elias and his wife Selma moved back into our apartment and ran the household as surrogate parents for those of us remaining at home. Before long, we began to go our separate ways.

My brother Elias was quite handsome and wanted to break into the movie business. Although he took acting lessons, nothing came of that ambition. He drifted into a career as a salesman, representing some of the manufacturers that supplied my father's textile business.

My brother Bernhard also began a career in textiles but soon changed direction. He established a base of clients to whom he sold textile items on the installment plan and visited them weekly to deliver orders and collect payments. However, his heart was not in textiles. He really wanted to go to the Mirrer Yeshiva in Poland to study and become a rabbi.

When Bernhard made the decision to leave for the Mirrer Yeshiva, he handed over his textile business to Elias, with the understanding that Elias would send him a stipend periodically to cover his living expenses. At the time, this arrangement was agreeable to Elias, who was not entirely satisfied with his job as a salesman. However, Elias later decided it was unfair that he had to do all the work and split the profits with Bernhard. They had an unfortunate falling out, ending their relationship. Elias retained the business, such as it was. Bernhard managed to obtain a visa for London, where he found employment as a rabbi.

My brother Jonas was the only sibling steered by my parents toward a medical career. After finishing 10 years of earlier schooling, he began classes. However, Jonas was somewhat rebellious and stopped putting on *tefillin* (phylacteries) in the morning. My parents were greatly disappointed when they discovered this and stopped paying tuition for his continued medical education. While they were prepared to educate a doctor, they were not about to do so when he was abandoning Jewish traditions and observances. Ironically, Jonas would not have had the opportunity to bring his studies to a successful conclusion in any case, as increasingly stringent Nazi restrictions blocked Jewish students from attending universities.

My youngest brother, Josef, who was born in 1920, was unable to complete even his basic elementary education due to the antisemitic policies in Germany at the time. When he was approximately 15 years old, Josef ran away from home, claiming that his brothers constantly ganged up on him and made his life at home unbearable. He later showed up in Calcutta, India, where he built a successful shipping agency business.

My sister Fannie started a small business selling ladies' dresses and coats. She would travel to Berlin to buy over-runs and irregular items from garment manufacturers and then sold them from her home. Her business strategy was to advertise one garment at a time in the classified section of the newspaper. After Fannie married, she and her husband Izzy used two rooms of their apartment as stockrooms for her business. Izzy dealt in used canvas sacks that he cleaned, repaired, and then resold to the trade. This was a filthy business and a constant source of friction between them. Fannie wanted Izzy to give it up, but he refused since it was quite profitable.

Fannie and Izzy eventually separated. Fannie went with their son, Manfred, to Yugoslavia, where they lived on a farm with assumed non-Jewish identities. After the war, Fannie moved to Manchester, England, where Izzy was living, but they never reunited. She returned to the business of selling dresses from Germany, and he took up his old sack and bag business.

Sali was the tallest of my sisters. She had beautiful blond hair and blue eyes. In fact, she was the "spitting image" of what the Nazis described as the ideal female of their "Master Race." But, of course, Sali was Jewish.

Sali married Wilhelm Krausz and opened a ladies' clothing shop in Leipzig on Petersstrasse, a busy thoroughfare with many upscale retail shops. During the war, Sali, her husband, and their 5-year-old son, Ernst, disappeared without leaving a trace. We clung to the hope that the worst had not happened, but they were never heard from again.[1]

Although I was on good terms with all my siblings, I felt closest to Hilda. She most resembled my mother in character and appearance. Hilda attended *Die Möringsche Handelsschule*, a trade school that taught secretarial skills, and then secured employment as a secretary for a Jewish company.

Hilda met and married a dashing young man named Max, who

---

1. Wilhelm, Sascha (Sali), and 5-year old Ernst were deported to the Riga ghetto on January 21, 1942. Wilhelm was later deported to the Auschwitz III-Monowitz forced labor camp, where he died on September 29, 1944.

impressed me for two reasons: He had a mustache, and he rode a motorcycle with an attached sidecar. Professionally, he was a furrier, in business for himself. Max and I went each week to *Gemorah shiurim* (Talmud lessons), which were taught at the Agudah *shul*.

Meanwhile, I had begun to take an interest in girls. I met a girl by the name of Dorle. While we seemed to enjoy each other's company, there was no real commitment. When she decided to go for a year on *Hachshara* (training) to prepare herself for immigration to Palestine and asked if I would wait for her, I had no immediate reply. While I was contemplating my response, my sister-in-law Selma came to me with a suggestion that changed my life forever.

Selma, who had managed to maintain ties with her family during these difficult times, had returned from attending her cousin's bar mitzvah in Berlin with news to share. At the event, she had met a young lady in whom she felt I would be interested and suggested that I travel to Berlin to meet her. There was a special excursion train with a reduced round trip fare from Leipzig to Berlin on Sundays. Selma encouraged me to go as soon as possible.

I decided that I would go to Berlin the following Sunday if I could still get a ticket. I thought to myself, *It would make a nice day. What have I got to lose?* I asked Selma, "What is her name?"

She replied, "Martha Weinreb."

Martha Weinreb, 1936

Photograph in the editors' private collection

CHAPTER TWO
Nuremberg to Berlin

Martha narrates:

I was born on May 23, 1919, at Wolkernstrasse number 39, in Nuremberg, Germany. I was the third of nine children. My older siblings were named Eva and Leo. In birth order, my younger siblings were named Sophie, Sigmund, Josef, Jenny, Lazarus ("Lulu"), and Benno. We were all born in Nuremberg except Benno, who was born after we moved to Berlin.

My father's parents, Abraham and Hinda Weinreb, were born in Galicia. They immigrated to Germany and lived in Fürth, an extended suburb of Nuremberg. They had seven children and established a wholesale art and picture framing business. I remember their hospitality and beautiful home, where they often invited travelers who passed through town to join them for *Shabbos* (Sabbath).

Much of our large, extended family lived in Nuremberg. I especially remember my Uncle Simche and Aunt Sali (my mother's sister) and their five children: Leo, Mali, Sigmund, Refoel and Mina. Unfortunately, Uncle Simche lost both legs in a train accident. After that, their lives were difficult. Their son Leo took charge of the family textile business, and one of the children was sent to Berlin to live for a time with our grandparents to make it easier for *Tante* (aunt) Sali to cope.

My mother's parents, Rabbi Moses and Rachel Rottenberg, were born in Kurima, Hungary. They lived in Berlin at Blumenstrasse number 21. When we moved to Berlin in 1928, we lived closer to them and nearby my aunts, Mali, Toni and Jenny, and their families.

Both of my parents worked very hard. Before their marriage, my mother owned a millinery shop, where she applied her talents and flair in hat design to creating beautiful hats for an appreciative private clientele. She had a natural ability for the business, which continued to thrive after she and my father married and he was serving under Franz Joseph, Kaiser of Austria and King of Hungary, in the Austro-Hungarian Army (commonly called the K&K Army).

After my father was honorably discharged from the army, he started building a business as a wine and liquor merchant in Nuremberg. This involved a great deal of travel to establish a client base. As the economic situation declined and circumstances necessitated a move to a more Jewish neighborhood with better schools, my parents began to debate the pros and cons of moving to Berlin.

They made the decision while I was away for a short vacation at the *Kinderheim* (children's camp) in Bad Kissingen, a spa near Fürth. When my father came on his motorcycle to pick me up, he told me we were moving. After taking leave of our family in Fürth, we returned to Nuremberg, and my parents settled their affairs. We said goodbye to our family in Nuremberg and were off by train to Berlin, the city that was to become our home for the next eleven years. The move was especially hard for me because we were leaving behind so much of our family.

Before my parents could start organizing their business in Berlin, they had to find an apartment large enough to accommodate our family. This was difficult, as many landlords were not interested in tenants with large families. Finally, my parents avoided mentioning the size of our family, and their application was accepted. We settled into our new apartment at Ritterstrasse number 111. The location was not ideal because it was not near my grandparents' house, but it was large enough to meet our needs. There were numerous bedrooms and a long corridor that was wide enough for the children to play and even ride a scooter.

My older sister, Eva, and I were enrolled in the *Kaiserstrasse*

Schule, a Jewish middle school that prepared students for high school. At school, I met a girl named Ilse, whose family had also relocated from Nuremberg. We became lifelong friends.

My grades were good. While my siblings went on to Jewish high schools, my parents sent me to the *Kleist Oberlyceum* (a tuition free school) to ensure that I would graduate with a high school certificate. Ultimately, I was denied the certificate because all Jewish students were made to leave these schools in 1936. I was 17 years old at the time.

These were hard times for our large family. As the situation for Jews worsened in Germany, it became increasingly difficult to make a living. My mother opened a produce shop, where I helped out after school. My father's business as a merchant required him to be away for much of the week. He would come home on weekends for *Shabbos*.

The *Shabbos* dinner table was the weekly high point of our family life. The hardships of the week vanished. The *Shabbos* table with its snowy white tablecloth and silver candlesticks was laden with delicious food prepared by my mother. I especially remember my father making sure that no crumbs were on the tablecloth. He would clean them off by raising the tablecloth slightly with the *challah* (bread) knife. To make sure we got into the proper *Shabbos* mood, my sister Eva, who was working by that time, would bring home delicious *Mozartkugeln* (chocolates) for all of us.

On Friday nights, we had a festive meal with *Kiddush* (blessing over wine), sang *zemiros* (Sabbath melodies), and discussed the happenings of the week. I remember my father's beautiful voice. He was often called to lead the *davening* (prayers) at a small *shul* nearby. On the High Holy Days, we went to a larger synagogue, the *Adas Yisroel*, on Siegmunds Hof. My brothers, Sigmund and Josef, who had inherited our father's wonderful voice, sang in the choir at a large synagogue on Oranienburgerstrasse in the east of Berlin. On *Shabbos*, they had to walk over an hour to get there.

As circumstances continued to change, we were forced to give up our large apartment. We moved to a street-level apartment at Flensburgerstrasse number 8. My mother's produce shop was located in front of our living quarters. Because Eva was working, I had more duties at home. I helped Lulu and Benno dress and get ready for school, took them to appointments, and sometimes transported Benno to school by having him sit on the package rack of my bicycle. My responsibilities also included delivering merchandise to customers and sometimes accompanying my mother to the fruit markets, where we selected fresh produce for our shop. Although we had to get up at 4:30 in the morning on those days, and I had to be in school on time, it was great fun.

My dear brother Leo left home to go to Palestine in 1934, when he was still a teenager. He returned to Europe during the years that followed and settled in Poland because he had a Polish passport. From that point on, our communication with Leo was spotty. However, he continued to correspond regularly with my sister Eva, who had married in 1937 and was living in Portugal.

During the war, Leo was in the Warsaw ghetto. According to a postcard he sent to Eva, dated July 6, 1942, Leo and his wife Bina were the parents of a 5-week-old daughter named Rachel. Eva sent Leo packages of clothing and food for the baby until she received a note from him saying they no longer needed baby things. Not long afterward, all communication from Leo stopped.[1]

---

1. The Warsaw ghetto uprising ended on May 16, 1943. Records in the German Federal Archives state that Leo died in the Majdanek concentration camp in June 1943. According to surviving family members, Bina and Rachel died in the ghetto.

By the mid-1930s, the need to leave Germany had become urgent, as anti-Jewish sentiment and oppressive Nazi policies made it increasingly difficult to live and work normally. My mother and father insisted I learn a trade that would help me financially if I ever had a chance to emigrate. I was enrolled in a fashion school called the *Mode Schule Knolle* to learn fashion sketching and design.

My first job was as an apprentice with an atelier for fancy toddler and girls' dresses. I obtained the position through the recommendation of Frau Ascheim, a good friend of our family. Although the job paid only pocket money, I was happy for the hands-on experience in dressmaking. In my spare time, I tutored the Ascheim's 6-year-old daughter Renate and helped her with her schoolwork.

My next position was as an apprentice at a dressmaking establishment called *Mode Salon Link*. While I received minimum pay, my skills continued to improve. I was pleased with my progress.

Throughout this time, I kept in contact with my two dear friends, Ilse and her cousin Margot. The three of us were very close. We were called "*das kleeblatt*" (the three-leaf clover). We got together as often as we could, and our friendship remained very strong until we were separated by circumstances.

Ilse immigrated to Buenos Aires. After the war, she located me through the Red Cross. Years later, during a trip with her husband to the United States, she visited me in New York. It was a very emotional experience for both of us. Sadly, Ilse was murdered in her home in Buenos Aires by an intruder.

Margot moved to California. We found each other through a mutual acquaintance and continued to correspond for a while. Unfortunately, we did not remain connected. Life simply took over.

In 1937, at the bar mitzvah party of my cousin Izzy, I met Selma Isaak, a new member of our extended family. She was visiting from

Leipzig and suggested that I meet her brother-in-law, who also lived in Leipzig. Conveniently, there was a round trip excursion train from Leipzig to Berlin on Sundays that he could take to meet me. Selma asked if I was agreeable to a meeting, to which I responded, "Why not? What is his name?"

She replied, "Pinkas Isaak."

OUR STORY: MARTHA & PINKAS ISAAK

CHAPTER THREE
Berlin – And So We Met

Pinkas narrates:

I arrived at the Anhalter *Bahnhof* (railway station) in Berlin on a beautiful, sunny Sunday morning in May 1937. As soon as was reasonable given the early hour, I called the number my sister-in-law Selma had given to me and spoke with Martha. We agreed to meet at 2:00 pm at the *Stadt* (City) *Bahnhof* Bellevue, which was near her home at Flensburgerstrasse number 8. To be sure we would recognize each other, we described what we looked like and what we would be wearing. I had on a very nice jacket that I had borrowed from my brother Elias in order to impress the girl I was about to meet.

Martha had explained that the nearest station to Bellvue was *Tiergarten* (zoo). When the train stopped at the *Tiergarten* station, I got off, thinking this was the station she meant. It wasn't. As a result, I had to take a half-hour walk through the park to get there. This made me late for our appointment. Since Martha did not want to be seen waiting, she had crossed the street to see who would turn up. Finally, we got together and went to a coffee shop to sit down and talk.

I never found anyone easier to talk to than Martha, but she had only one hour before she needed to leave for an appointment with a girl she was tutoring. She said she could meet me again at 4:00 that afternoon, which gave me more time to walk around and become acquainted with the neighborhood.

When Martha and I met again later that day, it was almost time for me to go to the train station for my return trip to Leipzig, so we walked in that direction. We were both attracted to each other and would have liked for time to stand still, but, of course, time waits for no one. While

Martha urged me to walk faster, I hesitated. If anyone tells you there is no such thing as love at first sight, don't believe him. I held back because I felt that, if I caught this train, it would carry me out of her life forever. We arrived at the station just as the train was pulling out. "So sorry... What now?"

Because I did not want to attract too much attention to myself, Martha acted as my spokesperson. She booked a room for me at a local hotel for the night. Then I walked her home, and we agreed to meet again in the morning.

As I walked back to the hotel, I realized that I could be walking into a trap. So instead of continuing, I turned around and went to the park. I spent the night sitting on benches and walking around. I'll never understand why I thought I would be safer in the park at night than in a hotel. These were extraordinary times in Germany.

The next morning, I walked Martha to work and we met again that afternoon. After a few hours together, we reluctantly headed back to the train station. This time, I caught the train and left for Leipzig, but not before promising to come back again in two weeks, if only for a day trip. We exchanged letters, and I returned two weeks later and every second week thereafter.

As our relationship became more serious, Martha told her parents about me. They invited me to spend *Shabbos* with the family during my next trip to Berlin.

To get ready for this new stage in our relationship, I rented a room from two elderly German sisters who lived at Holsteiner Ufer number 2, near Martha's family. This arrangement would allow me to plan longer and more frequent visits to Berlin. Besides, I had no real job in Leipzig, given the circumstances for Jews at the time.

BERLIN – AND SO WE MET

Finally, the weekend I was to meet Martha's parents and family arrived. They lived in a small apartment in back of their shop. On Friday evening, I went to *daven* in the *shtiebel* (small synagogue) where Mr. Weinreb led the service. Afterward, he took me home and I met the rest of the family. They were the friendliest group waiting to meet me. We had a traditional Friday night meal with *zemiros* and conversation. After dinner, I was invited to sing the *Shir Hamaalos* before the *benching* (after-meal blessing). By sheer luck, I chose what they called "Papa's *Nigun*" (melody), which went over very well. After the meal, Mr. Weinreb and Martha walked me back to my room. I had the feeling that her parents approved of our deepening friendship.

If Martha's parents had any reservations about our relationship, there might have been three areas of concern. First, it had been only a short time since the wedding of their oldest daughter, Eva, and they might have needed some breathing space to recuperate. Second, they might have been concerned that I had no profession. Third, they might have wanted to obtain the approval of Martha's grandfather, Rabbi Moses Rottenberg, who would test and evaluate my religious knowledge and background. I decided to tackle the third concern first.

Two weeks later, I visited Rabbi Rottenberg. I must have passed the test and met his high standards, as he approved of our relationship. Another big plus in my favor was the hope that my brother, Rabbi Bernhard Isaak, who was by then living in London, would be able to find a sponsor for us to go to England. We all knew that Germany was a dangerous place without a secure future for Jews.

A few weeks later, we felt that it was time for Martha to come to Leipzig for a weekend to meet my family. My siblings liked her immediately. My father must have approved of her as well. While he had given each of my sisters 10,000 marks when they married and 5,000 marks to each of my brothers when they left the house, he did somewhat better for me.

Martha endeared herself to everyone. In February 1938, nine months after our first meeting, we became engaged with the approval of both families.

In the meantime, my future father-in-law had remained busy servicing his clientele. He was not seeking new customers but still had to attend to those on his established routes. Because of the anti-Jewish climate, he was uncomfortable using public transportation and decided to buy a motorcycle. If I remember correctly, it was a Zundapp 250cc.

When the dealer called to say the motorcycle was ready to be picked up, someone was needed to take delivery. I volunteered. When I arrived, he asked me if I knew how to ride a motorcycle. I replied, "Of course!"

He said, "OK, let me start it up for you." I sat on the motorcycle and he explained, "All you have to do now is move this little handle and you will be on your way." I asked him to show me how to stop, which he did. Then I was off.

Since this was a light motorcycle, no license was needed. I spent a few hours showing Mr. Weinreb how to operate it and even went with him on a one-day trip. I must say, he was a quick learner. He once let Martha and me use the motorcycle for a trip to Leipzig and back. It was an exciting three-hour trip each way, with a high adrenalin rush for both of us.

Time was moving on. We decided on a wedding date of September 4, 1938. In view of the increasingly tense situation, we agreed that it would be a low profile event. While waiting for the day to arrive, Martha visited me once in my rented room. A nosy neighbor felt it was his patriotic duty to inform the authorities. About an hour later, two

SA *(Sturm Abteilung)* soldiers knocked on the door, looking for me.[1]

My two German landladies answered the door and told them I was not there. Instead of barging in and looking for themselves, as was the standard procedure in those days, they left with the warning that I was to report to the police station as soon as I returned. We waited about an hour for the coast to clear and then left, never to return to that address again. I rented another room that was slightly larger and included kitchen privileges at Dortmunderstrasse number 4, located just over a small bridge on the other side of the River Spree.

We asked Rabbi Dr. Heinrich Cohn, a friend of the family, to perform the wedding ceremony at his synagogue on Lessingstrasse. He happily agreed. As it turned out, it was the last religious ceremony Rabbi Cohn conducted at the synagogue. Two months later, on November 9, 1938, during the terrible night called *Kristallnacht*, it was burned to the ground. Ours was possibly the last Orthodox wedding conducted in a synagogue setting in Berlin before the war.

Martha made a beautiful bridal gown for herself. On the day of the wedding, she hiked it up under her coat so she would not attract attention. She did not wear her veil as we walked quietly to the synagogue. Having had no experience in these matters, I purchased red instead of white roses for her bridal bouquet. In spite of all our apprehensions, we had a beautiful *chuppa* (wedding canopy) and ceremony and made it back to my in-laws' apartment without any disturbances.

The celebration was simple, with no music and only the immediate family in attendance. With her small car, my sister Fannie brought my father and sisters to Berlin. My sisters returned home after the wedding. My father stayed with us overnight and returned to Leipzig the next day.

---

1. SA soldiers (Storm Troopers) were sometimes referred to as Brownshirts, for the color of their uniform. They were known for acts of violent intimidation.

From one day to the next, the situation in Germany was becoming increasingly tense for all Jewish families, including ours. Everyone was trying desperately to find a way to escape the country. Some of our friends decided to go to Shanghai, which, at the time, was occupied by Japan and admitted Jewish immigrants. But somehow we could not see ourselves living in China, especially since we were hoping to receive British visas. We continued to look for another country where we could wait in the meantime.

After learning that Italy was still honoring Polish passports and would admit us with transit visas that showed a destination elsewhere, we met a man who, for a financial consideration, could obtain visas listing Japan or Paraguay as a final destination. With no intention of going to either of these countries, we picked Paraguay as a final destination, gave him 2000 marks to secure two transit visas, and entrusted him with our Polish passports. He assured us that he would mail them back to us, duly endorsed with a visa stamp.

To heat things up even more, the Polish government had decreed that the Polish passport of anyone who had been living outside of Poland for five years or more would be invalidated at the end of October. Nazi Germany responded with a hasty plan (the *Polenaktion*) to deport Jewish residents holding Polish passports.

Martha and I had Polish passports, even though both of us had been born in Germany. Like my father, my nationality was Polish. By her marriage to me, Martha's nationality was Polish as well.

On Friday, October 28, 1938, not even two months after our wedding, there was a knock at the door at 5:00 in the morning. Two policemen had come to arrest me. The *Polenaktion* (Poland Action) designed to rid the German Reich of Jewish residents had begun. I was told that I could bring a small suitcase and, most importantly, my Polish passport. When I told them I did not have my passport at the moment, they instructed Martha to bring it to the Alexanderplatz Police Station, where I was being taken. Then, with a spark of decency, they waited outside the door to let us say good-bye to each other.

Our passports were expected to arrive in the mail that morning. I told Martha that, whatever happened, she must not bring my passport to the police station. I hoped that these "precise" Germans would not deport me without my Polish passport but gave Martha an address in Krakow where she might find me if they decided to deport me anyway. I gave her all the money I had, and we took leave of each other, facing an uncertain future.

When I arrived at the police station, I found what seemed to be a hundred people milling around. By about two hours later, they all had been taken away and I was left there by myself, not sure what my fate would be. Before long, I was taken by patrol car to the police prison. There were about eighty people at the prison, all in the same situation: no passport. Through a friend, Martha was able to contact a lawyer who, for 1000 marks, found out where I was and promised to secure my release.

In the meantime, the first train of deportees had arrived at the Polish border, where its "passengers" were admitted. When the second train arrived and another after that, the Polish guards closed the border and refused to admit any more. After the border was closed, the deportees were discharged from the remaining trains in "No-Man's Land" between Germany and Poland, near the town of Zbaszyn, Poland.

All luggage and money over 10 marks per person were confiscated, and the empty trains were returned to Berlin. When word got back to the German officials, they realized that there was no purpose in sending any more trains. They ended the *Polenaktion* and released the Jews they were still holding, including me.

Later we learned that my father, Martha's father, and two of her brothers, Sigmund and Josef, had also been arrested. While we have been able to reconstruct what happened to Martha's father, all traces of her brothers and my father were lost.[2]

Martha narrates:

A few months after his arrest, my father was allowed to return home to settle his business affairs, but without Josef and Sigmund. Months later, when he attempted to flee with my mother to Hungary, she had the necessary visa but he did not. At the border, he was denied entry but insisted that my mother continue the journey. He was returned to Berlin. Not long after, Papa was arrested in *shul* (synagogue) while he was *davening* (reciting prayers) and taken to the Sachsenhausen concentration camp.[3]

Pinkas narrates:

For the moment, I was free to go. It was *Shabbos* afternoon, and I found myself on the street. I started walking back to our home to find Martha. Because we did not feel at all safe to remain on Dortmunderstrasse and hoped to offer comfort and support to the family, we moved to Martha's parents' apartment to be with her mother and remaining siblings. But this was only a short respite from terror.

---

2. Historical events and correspondence written by Sigmund and Josef strongly suggest that they were murdered in a forest near Kuršėnai, Lithuania, during the summer of 1941.

Alter Meier Isaak remains among the thousands whose fate immediately after their arrest and deportation has not been determined. Records in the Central Database of Shoah Victims' Names at Yad Vashem indicate that he was in Lodz, Poland, at some point during the war. The record states that he was murdered.

3. Noah Weinreb was murdered in the Sachsenhausen camp in May 1940.

About a week later, on Wednesday, November 9, 1938, there was feverish police activity and agitation in the streets. To avoid any trouble, we decided to go to Leipzig and stay there for a few days. But to our dismay, when the train we had boarded in Berlin that morning arrived in Leipzig, we looked out the window and saw that it was exactly like the station in Berlin. There were police and SA men milling about and questioning people. Petrified with fear, we ducked down low and hid on the train until it returned to Berlin the next morning

When we arrived back in Berlin, *Kristallnacht* had broken out in full force and fury. We hurried through the streets to get home, frightened and worried. We got there and discovered that bullets had shattered the window of the shop. Having nowhere else to go, we joined the family and spent the rest of the night with them, shivering in fright in the dark and cold. Finally, the fury abated, and an eerie calm settled over the city.

A few days later, early in the morning, two SA soldiers came to the apartment. Martha's sister Jenny saw them coming. She ran to our room and warned me to escape. I hastily dressed, and, without shoes, ran out the side door of the shop. Martha told me to go to the Ascheims, friends of the family whose daughter she had been tutoring. She would meet me there.

Although I left deep footprints in the snow, the soldiers did not bother to follow me. They were too busy breaking furniture and roughing up the girls and younger boys, Lulu and Benno. When they finally left, Martha came to meet me. Realizing that we needed to leave as soon as possible, the Ascheims gave me some breakfast and, most importantly, the address of a travel agent who might be able to help us.

Martha and I made our way to the address the Ascheims had given us. The travel agent verified that Italy would admit us if we could show that we had a visa for another country as our destination. He had a friend in Venice who had run a travel agency in Vienna until it was closed down when the Nazis marched into Austria. He recommended that we look him up for further assistance. We prepared to leave Germany without delay.

We bought rail tickets for December 2, 1938. Then we sent two small suitcases by Rail Express to my brother Bernhard in London and came up with a plan to send Martha's wedding rings to him as well. I had given Martha a gold wedding ring and a diamond ring that I inherited from my mother. Because of the current atmosphere in Germany, she wore instead only a cheap replica wedding band.

We bought a box of chocolates, dug out the cream from one of the candies, and put both good rings inside. Then we carefully tucked the chocolate back into its silver foil, re-wrapped the box in brightly decorated Christmas paper, and mailed it to Bernhard, along with a carefully worded greeting card. The package arrived safely, and Martha still has the rings.

Martha's mother and remaining siblings came to the train station to see us off and wish us a safe trip. We made two more stops in Germany before leaving the country. The first stop was in Nuremberg to say goodbye to our family there. The second stop was in Munich, where Martha's cousin Sigmund lived. Sigmund worked for a Jewish organization, assisting the few people who had been released from a local concentration camp. On December 4, 1938, he went with us to the train station, where we boarded the train for Venice.

Much to our surprise, the procedures at the German border control, which had been of much concern and a great source of apprehension, took place without incident. The train stopped again at the Italian border, where the guards waved us on after a cursory look at our endorsed passports. We had passed safely through the first stage of our journey.

Our next stop was Venice.

OUR STORY: MARTHA & PINKAS ISAAK

CHAPTER FOUR
Venice

Pinkas narrates:

We arrived in Venice early in the morning with a total of 20 German marks between us. We looked forward with both hope and trepidation to our meeting with the man who would be our benefactor. We changed our money into Italian *lire* and took a *vaporetto* (water bus) to the Lido. The address was 14 Via Marcantonio Bragadin, Lido di Venezia. The sign on the door read "Villa Di Brioni." It's funny how these minute details stay in one's mind, almost seventy years later.[1]

It seems that the travel agent in Berlin had called his friends, Mr. and Mrs. Brisky, as they appeared to have been expecting us. When we knocked on the door, they welcomed us into their house and invited us to join them for supper. After supper, they suggested that, since we must be exhausted from our trip, we should go up to our room, get a good night's sleep, and tell them all about our situation in the morning.

Over breakfast the next day, we told them our story. We thanked them for their hospitality and explained that we would need to look for other accommodations because we were unable to pay for our room and board at this time. We thought this might be possible with the help of Jewish organizations.

They replied that, since our stay in Italy would be short, we should stay with them and worry about payment later. We gratefully accepted their offer. I knew we would be able to repay them eventually since I had been able to transfer part of the money my father had given to me when Martha and I became engaged to my brother Bernhard. He was living in London, and the funds were available.

---

1. The villa still stands at this address. Its current name is Villa Angelica.

Our stay in Italy was relatively short. In less than six weeks, the British Consulate in Venice notified us that we should come in to apply for our visas. When we arrived, the clerk suggested that we might be better off applying at the Chief Consulate in Milan, as they had greater authority. We did as he suggested.

In Milan, we presented our two passports but were shocked to discover that the permit did not include Martha. While the consul commiserated with us, he could not overstep his authority. At this news, Martha burst out in tears, and I stated that I would not go by myself. I had forgotten that I was still single when my brother and the sponsor who supported the application had applied. Thus, when the document came through, it was only for me.

The consul excused himself for a few minutes to consult with other members of his staff. When he returned, he asked for the two passports and, with a smile and a flourish, stamped first one and then the other, enabling England to admit Mr. and Mrs. Isaak.

To avoid a 14-day sea voyage, Martha and I decided to book a flight from Zurich to London. We were apprehensive because neither of us had ever flown in an airplane before. Then we returned to Venice to take leave of our hosts.

I asked Mr. Brisky for the cost of our stay. As we spoke, I was nervously toying with an automatic cigarette lighter that I had purchased in Germany as a souvenir. Mr. Brisky said that he had always wanted such a lighter and would accept it as full settlement of our bill. Our great regret is that we never contacted the Briskys from London, where we were overwhelmed by the circumstances and problems of settling in to our new life in a different country.

VENICE

**Villa Angelica, Lido, Venice, 2020
In 1938, known as the Villa Di Brioni**

Photograph used with permission, courtesy of the Noghera family
Website: www.villaangelica-venezia.com

OUR STORY: MARTHA & PINKAS ISAAK

CHAPTER 5
London

Pinkas narrates:

We arrived in London around the middle of January 1939. My brother met us at the airport and took us to the room he had rented for us near Whitechapel Road. Then we went out to get something to eat before returning to our accommodations for the night. We were appalled by the poor living conditions, especially when compared to the sanitary conditions in Berlin. There was no toilet. One made do with an outhouse in the yard. And, while there was a bathtub, the owners used it to store coal.

In the morning, the homeowners heard us moving around and asked what we needed. Martha wanted to know where we could wash. They responded by bringing us two milk bottles filled with water and a washbasin.

For lunch, Bernhard took us to a kosher delicatessen called Bloom's, where we had enormous corned beef sandwiches that were bigger than we could ever imagine. This was a special treat since, for the last few years, there had been no kosher meat except chicken available in Germany. In Italy, we did not even have chicken.

After lunch, our first concern was to find another room. Any other accommodation would be an improvement over our first night's lodging. We applied for assistance from a Jewish organization at Bloomsbury House.[1] They gave us a small weekly stipend and provided Martha with some material to make a maternity dress, as she

---

1. Bloomsbury House, a former hotel on Bloomsbury Street, was the headquarters for many Jewish aid organizations that did what they could to ease the lives of newly arrived refugees.

was pregnant. I looked for an entry-level position in the garment industry and found myself a job with H. Lass & Company, a business that made greatcoats (overcoats) for the British army.

As our lives settled into an uneasy routine, we remained very concerned about immediate family members remaining in Berlin. We found a position as an *au pair* for Martha's sister Sophie, which enabled her to obtain a valid entry visa to England. Martha's sister Eva and her husband succeeded in obtaining entry visas to Portugal, first for Jenny and somewhat later for *Mutti* (Martha's mother). We then worked on finding a solution for Leslie and Ben.

Here I must note that our survival and the plan described below, which resulted in the rescue of eight boys from Germany, would not have been possible without the very vigorous involvement of my late brother, Rabbi Bernhard Isaak. We are immensely grateful to him. Without his assistance, none of us would be here today.

Bernhard and I devised a plan that we hoped would bring Martha's youngest brothers, Leslie and Benno, and perhaps other children to London. Bernhard was acquainted with the Chassidic Sassover *Rebbe* (Rabbi), who worked with his disciples and Bernhard to establish a youth hostel for refugee children in a small house provided by the *Rebbe*. Then we created stationery with an "official" letterhead, on which we typed letters accepting responsibility for the children we hoped to save. Our plan was to meet the boys at the airport, where we would present the letter to the British authorities as assurance that the children had been brought to England responsibly.

To test the plan and see whether it would work, we mailed one of these letters to *Mutti*. The letter stated that the hostel was willing to accept Leslie and would be responsible for his education and care. We explained to *Mutti* that, if she could somehow get Leslie on a flight to London, we would meet the plane and present the letter to the authorities to get him admitted.

Mutti agreed to the plan and, with great courage, managed to dispatch Leslie on a plane bound for London. The next day, we received a call from an official at Croydon Airport. The caller said they had an 11-year-old boy who could not speak English and had arrived with only a German child's identification card and a letter. They asked that someone come to pick him up. Putting the final step of our plan into action, we retrieved Leslie from the airport and brought him to the youth hostel, where Martha and I had moved in anticipation of his arrival.

It should be noted that the *Kinderausweis* (a German child's photo-identification card) that Leslie carried was not an international travel document. It was miraculous that, on the strength of our letter alone, the plan worked. Mutti and all the other ladies who followed in her footsteps deserve the highest praise for having the strength, courage, and determination to send their children on a plane to England, not knowing for certain what the outcome would be.

After our success in getting Leslie out of Germany, we repeated the same procedure for our youngest brother, Benno. He also was admitted to England. Encouraged by this, we sent similar letters for Martha's two cousins, Bob and Gerson. When they landed successfully, we wrote letters for two young brothers, the children of family friends. Then we wrote letters for two boys from Czechoslovakia sponsored by the Sassover *Rebbe*.

Our last two letters were for Martha's cousins, Yossi and Izzy. Sadly, their mother was unable to send them. All three disappeared in the Holocaust.

Further efforts to get children out of Germany with the use of the letters came to a halt when the British Home Office became suspicious of our activities. They informed us that nobody further would be admitted without a visa issued by a consulate from the country of departure. By that time, we had eight children in the youth hostel, where Martha and I acted as house parents, with expenses paid by a Jewish organization.

While the Sassover *Rebbe* who had assisted us did not deny admittance to any of the children based on their level of religious observance, he did urge the boys to have their hair cut short and grow *payes* (side curls). This was particularly difficult for the boys who came from Jewish households that held different perspectives.

Martha narrates:

During our time in the hostel, we tried to create a home for these eight children. Before the first *Shabbos,* the *Rebbe* gave me £10 (British pounds) and said, "Go, make *Shabbos* for the children." In those days, 10 pounds was a substantial sum. I cooked for *Shabbos* and much more with that money.

Many years later, completely by chance, we met one of the now grown children in a delicatessen where we had stopped to eat during a day of shopping in Brooklyn, New York. He recognized us, though he had not seen us since childhood, and we had all grown much older.

Similarly, and again by chance, our niece met one of the "boys" at the wedding of her granddaughter in Jerusalem. He was the grandfather of the groom. What a coincidence! When he realized that she was related to us, he praised Pinkas and related how the children had escaped Germany and come to London with the help of those letters. He spoke of the time we had spent together in the hostel, though our stay there was short. So many years had passed, yet we all remembered.

LONDON

Pinkas narrates:

The war situation had become increasingly dire. England was ill prepared for the war. We vividly remember two scenes: the British Home Guard training in the streets with broomsticks in their hands because they did not have rifles and the countless barrage balloons flying very high over London.[2]

The government decided to evacuate all school children from London, which meant the hostel had to be closed. The plan was to send the children to small communities outside the city, where they would be taken care of by families who were willing to take them into their homes for the duration of the emergency. In other words, where a child ended up was arbitrary and unpredictable.

We tried not to take that chance with Leslie and Benno. Martha's cousin in Manchester put us in touch with two Jewish families in Gateshead. They were prepared to take in the boys for the duration of the emergency. We bought tickets for Leslie and Benno to go to Gateshead but could not accompany them. I was working in a factory that paid me £3.10 a week, and Martha was in the third trimester of her pregnancy.

We had made arrangements for Martha to go the Lord Bearstead Jewish Memorial Hospital when the time came for the baby to be born, but it did not work out that way. The government evacuation order included pregnant women. My brother Bernhard was the rabbi at the New Road Synagogue. The cantor at the Synagogue recommended that Martha go to Llanelli, a small coal-mining village in Wales where his parents lived, and there was a small Jewish community.

As we were making plans for Martha to go to Llanelli, there was

---

2. Barrage balloons were very large, hydrogen-filled silver balloons, tethered with steel cables. These cables posed a severe collision risk to Germany's attacking aircraft, making their approach much more difficult.

a knock on the door. We opened the door and were shocked to find Leslie and Benno standing there. The boys explained that, although their hosts were nice and treated them well, the level of religious observance in their homes was unfamiliar. At Leslie and Ben's insistence, their hosts purchased train tickets for the boys to return to London. When they arrived, they simply showed up at our door, and that was that.

What now? We enrolled the boys in the Jewish Free School in London, but that solution was short-lived. With steadily worsening war conditions in London and evacuation orders that extended to the entire city in effect, The Jewish Free School was forced to close its doors.

The government order to "Evacuate Forthwith" was issued at 11:07 a.m. on Thursday, August 31, 1939. It marked the beginning of Operation Pied Piper.[3] Few realized that, within a week, so many Londoners would have a new address.

All of the schoolchildren were issued gas masks and evacuated as a group to Chelmsford, which was located in the countryside outside of London. We hoped that Leslie and Benno might be placed with Jewish families, but that was not to be. The buses were met by volunteer social workers, who introduced the children to host families. Leslie and Benno were placed with a very nice, well-meaning Gentile family that even had the boys accompany them to church on Sunday.

We were concerned and contacted Rabbi Cohn, who had officiated at our wedding, which now seemed long ago. Rabbi Cohn had also emigrated from Berlin. He managed to get the boys placed in a Jewish hostel in Ely, about 40 miles outside of London. They remained in Ely until after Leslie's bar mitzvah.

---

3. Operation Pied Piper refers to the evacuation of millions, mostly children, from cities to more rural areas to protect them from aerial bombings by Nazi Germany.

OUR STORY: MARTHA & PINKAS ISAAK

CHAPTER SIX
Llanelli, Wales

Martha narrates:

My sister-in-law Hilda and her little daughter Miriam had come to London to wait for immigrant visas to the United States. Hilda's husband Max was already in New York, where he had been admitted on a business visa and was working on obtaining visas for his wife and daughter to join him. It was a lengthy and time-consuming process, since the U.S. quota system was designed to limit immigration.

On the September 3, 1939, Prime Minister Churchill declared war on Germany. A few days later, London was bombed and panic followed. School children were evacuated, and pregnant mothers were advised to get out of London. I was eight months pregnant.

Pinkas' sister Hilda and her 2-year-old daughter Miriam were living with us at the time of the evacuation. A friend provided Hilda with an address in Llanelli, a small town in Wales. (The name of the town is pronounced "Hlah-neth-lee"). We were happy for Hilda to have found a Jewish family who could help her. Without additional communication, Hilda and Miriam left for Llanelli.

Meanwhile, I had registered with a maternity hospital in London, in preparation for the birth of our baby. Of course, we had not expected the war. With the turn of events, Pinkas and I decided that I would follow Hilda to Llanelli by myself, since he could not leave his job. He said my safety and that of our baby was the priority.

When Hilda arrived in Wales, she managed to rent a room with a double bed in the house of a coal miner and his family. It looked very clean and comfortable. When I arrived a few days later, Hilda was able to secure a small room in the same house for me. The room was very small, with just enough space for a bed and a chair. But the knowledge that Hilda was nearby gave me confidence that everything would be okay.

A few days and sleepless nights went by. I began to worry about my condition and thought about returning to London. Hilda would not hear of it without consulting a doctor. There was no hospital in this small town. Instead, there were nurses and midwives who went to patients' houses to render medical services, including assistance with childbirth. Doctors were only available in special circumstances.

On September 11, 1939, a doctor came to the house and, after an examination, told me to stay in bed because he expected me to give birth in a few hours. Because I was healthy and strong, he said I should not worry. Still, I felt frightened and desperate. I could only think, *Which bed? Which room?* Hilda immediately offered me her room and bed. "Everything will be alright," she said. And so it was.

Hilda saw me through this unexpected but joyful situation, with little Miriam waiting outside the bedroom, listening intently for the sound of a baby's cry. Suddenly, I became calm, optimistic, and confident that everything was in G-d's hands and would be all right.

Our baby was born that day. Pinkas was completely unaware of this, as there was no telephone in the house. Worried about the imminent birth, he sent a telegram suggesting I come back to London. I responded with a telegram that said, "MOTHER AND SON DOING WELL." I'm sure he was shocked. He took the train to Wales to see his new son and make arrangements for the *bris* (Jewish rite of circumcision).

There were few resources where we were staying, but we made the best of it. There was no *mohel* (a person who performs the circumcision) in Llanelli, but the local Jewish families arranged for a *mohel* to come from nearby Cardiff. They also provided baby gifts and prepared a small collation for the *bris*, which was set up in the kitchen.

Pinkas managed to arrive a couple of days before the *bris*, and we all crowded into the two small rooms. I was not allowed out of bed for more than a few minutes, as was customary in those days.

At the *bris*, the baby was named *Moshe Dovid*, the Hebrew name of both our grandfathers. A few days later, we went to the town hall to register the birth of our son, Morris David Isaak. The registrar emphasized proudly that, since our son was born in Wales, he was Welsh, not British. Not feeling very patriotic at the moment, I thought to myself, *This baby has escaped from Germany, just endured the ordeals of birth, and is healthy and beautiful. As far as I'm concerned, he's neither Welsh nor British. He's Jewish.*

Pinkas returned to his job in London shortly after the *bris*. A few days later, accompanied by Hilda and Miriam, I returned with my baby to our flat on Philpot Street.

OUR STORY: MARTHA & PINKAS ISAAK

CHAPTER SEVEN
Back in Wartime London

Pinkas narrates:

For economic reasons and because we ultimately planned to go to America, I feel we never really put down roots in England. During our stay, we moved from the one-room flat on Brick Lane to Philpot Street and other addresses described in this chapter. Throughout our time in England, the size of our living quarters was the only factor limiting how many people we were able to accommodate and shelter.

As we continued to welcome newly arrived family members, including Hilda and Miriam, the flat on Philpot Street became too small. We stayed there until after our new son's *pidyon ha-ben* (a Jewish ceremony of redemption that takes place when a first-born son is one month old). The meal at the event was graciously provided by my brother Elias and his wife Selma, who also had managed to emigrate from Leipzig and were living in London.

After the *pidyon ha-ben*, Hilda watched the baby while we looked for a larger flat in a better neighborhood. We found a top-floor, two-bedroom flat in a house on Egerton Road in Stamford Hill. The house had an Anderson shelter, which was an advantage. The Anderson shelter, a small hut made of corrugated steel, was provided and installed in the back yard by the government. For safety in the event of an air raid, the hut was installed partially below ground. Hilda and Miriam stayed with us for a few months until their visas came through, and they left for New York

The war had begun in earnest. There were German air raids and bombings nearly every night. When the air raid siren sounded, we had to go into the Anderson shelter and remain there until we heard the "all-clear" signal. It was a trying time for everyone, despite valiant attempts by Mr. Churchill to bolster morale by reminding us with posters and radio broadcasts to "Keep Calm and Carry On." The nightly ritual was especially memorable. Every evening, after his supper and bath, we had to wrap Moish (Morris David) in a blanket, put him in a laundry basket, and take him with us to the shelter.

The small shelter was quite crowded, with our landlord's family, the three of us, and Bernhard, who joined us there every night. The only alternative to this would have been to spend the night in the nearby Underground (subway station), which was equipped with bunk beds. This was not a good option for us, so we continued to stay in the small shelter during the nightly air attacks on London, known as the "blitz." Every night, Germany's V-1 rockets rained down on the city, leaving frightening views of London burning in their wake. At the time, Leslie and Benno were still living outside of London in Ely.

We eventually looked for relief from this difficult situation by joining a group led by Rabbi Julius Jacobowitz, who had befriended us. We went with them to Shefford to be with the small Jewish community there.[1] We were unable to find accommodations in Shefford but were able to rent rooms in Meppershall, a small village nearby, from a man called Captain Bell. Bernhard took a room there as well. The Captain was a retired naval officer and a fine gentleman. He lived alone in this big house with a beautiful dog, an Irish Setter named Barney.

Barney insisted on making friends with me. Because of my job, I could not stay in Meppershall. Instead, I traveled from London to visit every third or fourth weekend. While the bus from London to

---

[1]. Rabbi Julius Jacobowitz's son Immanuel became the Chief Rabbi of England. He was knighted by the Queen in 1981 and titled Lord Rabbi Jacobowitz. Later, he became the Rabbi of the Fifth Avenue Synagogue in New York City.

Shefford ran every two hours, the local bus from Shefford to Meppershall ran only twice a day. When I arrived in Shefford on a Friday afternoon, I could not wait for the bus to Meppershall because the hour was late and *Shabbos* would soon begin. Instead, I would set out on foot. How he knew I was coming to visit I'll never know, but Barney always met me halfway. Full of joy, he accompanied me back to the house.

That spring, Martha's sister Eva, who was still in Portugal, notified me that their father, Noah Weinreb, had died on May 3, 1940, in a German concentration camp. While Leslie and Benno were informed right away of his passing because they had to say *Kaddish* (the Jewish prayer for the deceased), I did not tell Martha and Sophie until after the 30-day period of *shloshim*, so they would not have to observe a full *shivah* (7-day formal period of mourning).[2]

After many months of living apart and watching the sky light up every night with the red flames of London burning, Martha became increasingly concerned about my safety and welfare. As soon as the frequency of air raids seemed to have diminished, she decided to move back to London so we would at least be together. We rented a house at 4 East Bank in Stamford Hill. Here we had much more room and planned for Benno and Leslie to stay with us when they came home from Ely.

Martha narrates:

When they returned to London, my brothers moved in with us. They set up a workbench in the house to repair and create jewelry, since they wanted to be skilled as jewelers when their hope of immigrating to the United States materialized. While waiting for their American

---

2. The Orthodox Jewish tradition stipulates that the *Kaddish* prayer is to be recited by male mourners in a quorum of ten or more.

quota numbers to come up so they could apply for visas, Leslie volunteered for service in the British army. Having already suffered the loss of our fathers, my three brothers, and Pinkas' sister Sali and her family, I felt that my two surviving brothers should not be placed in harm's way in the British Army during wartime. However, it was Leslie's choice to become a British soldier. Pinkas petitioned to cancel Leslie's enlistment, but the judge at Hackney Magistrate Court denied his request. Despite our fears and apprehensions, we understood that perhaps Leslie needed to do this because of all the turmoil in his young life.

In the meantime, Sophie stayed on with the family who had sponsored her as an *au pair*. Through Bernhard, she was introduced to a young man named Louis. After a short courtship, they became engaged and were married at Silverstein's Restaurant on White Chapel Road. I was very pleased and proud that Sophie wore the gown I had made for my own wedding. Later, two other girls were married in that same gown.

Pinkas narrates:

They say that one gets used to everything. In spite of air raids nearly every night, our lives continued. We had hoped to have more than one child, but this wish was not to be granted. After three miscarriages, for which our doctors at the time had no solution, Martha and I became resigned to the likelihood that we would not have a larger family. We enrolled Moish, who was now 3-years old, in a private kindergarten.

As for me, an opportunity for a new business venture surfaced. Bernhard had met a gentleman by the name of Ostreicher, a chemist who had a rudimentary knowledge of how to make torch (flashlight) batteries. Bernhard decided to go into business with him. When they opened a factory to manufacture batteries, I joined them. While we realized that we could not compete with established companies that were busy filling large government orders for the military, we reasoned that the blackout conditions in England had created an enormous civilian need for torch batteries. We named the factory "Dawn Products" and marketed the batteries under the brand name "Millicent," after a niece of the man who had loaned us money to get the business started.

At about that time, the Polish government-in-exile, which was based in London under General Andersen, was enlisting men of Polish background for a special army unit to fight alongside the British Army. I was not about to allow myself to be drafted into the Polish Army, which was known to be virulently antisemitic. They even had this reputation during peacetime conditions before the war. It was rumored that some of their Jewish conscripts did not survive their two-year enlistment but died in suspicious accidents or from "friendly" fire.

Fortunately, England had a law that exempted certain groups from conscription into the special army unit. One group in this category was theology students. I enlisted at a yeshiva as an outside student, which gave me that protection.

We continued to live as normal a life as the times allowed. We enrolled Moish in the *Yesodei Hatorah* School in Stamford Hill and bought a second-hand car, a Standard, which gave us good service in spite of being 13 years old. The only problem with the car was its frequent flat tires, which actually needed to be replaced. However, the purchase of new tires was not allowed during wartime. Petrol was also rationed, but we were entitled to a commercial allocation because of our factory.

We became friendly with a family whose daughter was one year older than Moish. Once a week, I got up at 5:00 in the morning to go to the butcher to pick up the weekly meat rations for both families. I always argued with the butcher over his reluctance to sell me beef hocks that Martha could use to make *galareta*, an aspic that is rich in protein. He refused to give them to me, always asking, "Don't you know there is a war on?" I always replied, "I know, but cows still have four legs." I suppose we were not important enough customers.

There was even entertainment. Once a week, we went to a cinema in Stoke Newington. For the entry fee of nine pence, we saw two movies and a newsreel that showed the events of the week. Our lives continued as such for a couple of years.

Sadly, there was to be no peace, either for London or for us. Under the direction of the German rocket scientist Werner Von Braun, who later surrendered to the Americans and went on to head-up rocket development in the United States, Hitler produced the first supersonic bombs, the V-2. These were actually long-range, pilot-less rockets that could attack during the day or night. The frightening thing about them was that you could not hear them coming. When they hit, you heard the explosions first. Only after the loud explosion did the shrieking whistle of the incoming rocket become audible.

We could see the frightening trail of the incoming rockets from our bedroom windows. At the time, Moish was attending school near our house in Amhurst Park. Whenever we heard an explosion, we rushed to the window to see if the school building was still standing. Like our neighbors, we lived with constant fear, apprehension, and uncertainty.

The city of London had installed bunk beds in the Underground stations, where citizens were urged to go for safety at night because there was not enough room to bed all of the city's residents in the "regular" shelters. Even in the Underground, it was important to arrive early to secure a bed. Latecomers had to find an available corner and sleep on the floor. Some were lucky enough to find a spot to sleep under the ping pong-sized protective steel tables that had been placed there for that purpose. Conditions in the shelters became a little more bearable when the trains stopped running, between 11 p.m. and 6 a.m.

Eventually, we tired of this nightly ordeal and decided to leave London for the relative calm of Manchester, where we had family that had emigrated from Nuremberg, Germany. We rented living space on Great Clewes Street. My brother Bernhard also decided to move temporarily to Manchester and rented a room nearby.

Our cousin, Sigmund Margulies, had been studying at a local yeshiva in Manchester. It was Sigmund who had accompanied us to the train station when Martha and I fled Germany in December 1938. He had enlisted in the British Army, where he was promoted to the rank of captain and spent his assignment with the British troops in India. Sigmund's brother, Rabbi Refoel Margulies, officiated at a *shul* in the nearby city of Hull and lived in Manchester with his wife Eva. Martha and their sister Mina became lifelong friends. Their brother Leo had been deported to the Buchenwald concentration camp.

When we returned to London sometime later, we rented the lower floor of a house at 91 Manor Road near Stoke Newington. We had two rooms, an eat-in kitchen, a bathroom, and the use of the garden in the back and the unfinished cellar. Given the available space, we bought an industrial sewing machine, which we installed in the cellar. Here, Martha could do some dressmaking. She took in work from a small dress factory, for which she was paid by the piece.

The war ended in 1945. Reflecting back on that time, a special event stands out. In 1946, we had the pleasure and honor of hosting a family gathering to welcome home Leo Margulies, who had survived five years in the notorious Buchenwald concentration camp. Instead of rejoining his family immediately after liberation, Leo stayed behind with a group of children who had survived but no longer had parents. He took them to France and stayed with them there until they all had been taken care of properly by Jewish organizations and individual sponsors.

Typical of his noble character, Leo delayed reuniting with his family until he was sure "his children," as he called them, were assured of good homes. We were happy and proud to be able to bring the whole family together for this significant celebration.

Leo was rewarded for his good deeds and caring when he immigrated to New York, married, and raised three sons who followed in his footsteps by leading lives permeated with Jewish tradition and learning.

Martha narrates:

One day, completely "out of the blue," as they say, we received a notice from the American Consulate in London, stating that our quota number had come up. We had almost forgotten that we applied for quota numbers to obtain American visas while we were still in Berlin. Our instructions were to get medical examinations and chest x-rays. We did so and placed the results in a large envelope on the mantelpiece, awaiting our appointment.

When the time came for our formal visa application, we were stunned to discover that Pinkas' visa could not be granted because his chest x-ray showed calcified spots that were diagnosed as traces of healed tuberculosis nodules. The consul assured us that this denial was not final. He said we could reapply at a later date without losing our place in the quota line. If a subsequent chest x-ray showed no further spread of the calcified nodules, there would be no reason to deny our application.

Needless to say, this was a devastating disappointment, but at least there was a small ray of hope. Because we had not anticipated a delay in obtaining our visas, we had sold many of our belongings in preparation for going to America.

We decided to go to Israel and spend the next waiting period in a more beneficial climate.

OUR STORY: MARTHA & PINKAS ISAAK

CHAPTER EIGHT
Israel

Martha narrates:

On our journey to Israel, we stopped in Holland to visit Pinkas' aunt and uncle and their daughter Fannie. *Onkel* (uncle) Chaim was the brother of Mindl Ehrenreich, Pinkas' mother. All three had survived several years in the Bergen-Belsen concentration camp where, heartbreakingly, another daughter and son perished. After the camp was liberated, they settled in The Hague, Holland, where *Onkel* Chaim and *Tante* (aunt) Lotte managed the Jewish community's *mikvah* (ritual bath), a job that provided them with living quarters. During our visit, we had the choice of seven bathrooms.

A humorous anecdote comes to mind. While in Holland, we passed a newsstand displaying Dutch comic books, similar to the American comics my twin nieces sent to Moish (David) when the girls and their parents lived in Lisbon, Portugal. Since their move to New York, they no longer sent packages containing Captain Marvel and Superman comics, and 10-year-old Moish missed them very much.

When Moish saw the Dutch comic books displayed at the newsstand, he wondered if they had any comics in English. He asked us to buy him some. We agreed, but only if he could negotiate the purchase by himself.

He must have been desperate because, after a moment's hesitation, he approached the man and asked, *"Haben Sie komische papieren für Englischer kinder?"* ("Do you have strange papers for English children?") We were completely surprised. While his German was awkward, we never thought Moish knew the language at all and wondered about all our "secrets" that he had heard and understood.

Pinkas narrates:

The trip from Holland to Tel Aviv in the newly established State of Israel was exhausting. It began with a long flight on a propeller-driven airplane to the airport in Haifa, Israel.[1] The flight was followed by a bumpy bus ride to Tel Aviv. In the heat and excitement, Martha suffered extreme motion sickness. When we reached Tel Aviv, we exchanged some British pounds for Israeli *lirot* at the exchange rate of one for one and were ready to begin the next chapter of our lives.

For the moment, our destination was the home of Martha's *Tante* Toni and *Onkel* Dov, where we had shipped a small crate containing our belongings prior to leaving England. Unfortunately, all of our family photographs were lost in transit from London to Israel. They were never recovered.

Tante Toni and *Onkel* Dov had two sons, Menachem and Alex. Menachem was an officer in the Irgun, the Israeli paramilitary force that fought against the British occupation until Israel's independence in 1948. He came home occasionally for an overnight stay. Their daughter Miriam was married.

Although their apartment was small, *Tante* Toni and her family welcomed us with open arms. They could not offer us a bedroom, so we had to bed down in the living room. In the bathtub, much to Moish's delight but certainly not to mine, a live carp swam around and around, awaiting its fate as *gefilte* (stuffed) fish for *Shabbos*. There was no room in the small icebox for a large carp. In Israel at the time, food was preserved in an icebox cooled by a heavy block of ice that was purchased daily from a wagon and carried home with special tongs.

Despite the crowded quarters and limited storage, we shared expenses and stayed with Toni and her family for almost six weeks. It was a priority for us to find our own accommodations.

---

1. Haifa airport (built in 1934) was the first international airport in Israel.

Finally, we settled into our own home, a small apartment at 3 Chever Haleumim Street, located right at the entrance to the Tel Aviv harbor. It was euphemistically called a one-bedroom apartment but was actually just one small room in a reconfigured office building. All of the tenants living on our floor shared a common toilet located on the floor below. On our floor, in a space originally intended for elevators, there were two showers that were used by all of the tenants living on the floor. It was all we could afford, and we still had to pay an additional 500 *lirot*, called "key money," to obtain it. "Key money" was commonly added as an incentive for a renting agent to locate a dwelling.

To its credit, the apartment had a window with a gorgeous view of the Mediterranean Sea beyond the harbor. In addition to affording a view and ventilation, the window proved useful in another way as well. When Martha wanted Moish, she would hang a towel out the window as a signal to him that it was time to come home from the beach where we used to go swimming.

Martha made our one-room apartment very cozy. The horizontal refrigerator we had shipped from England served as a kitchen counter. A two-burner electric hotplate and a sink and faucet in the corner completed our kitchen. We bought a table and four chairs, a daybed with a pullout trundle bed for us, and a horizontal Murphy bed for Moish. Over his bed, we built a small cabinet with glass doors to store and display our silver candlesticks and some knick-knacks. This was our home, where we lived until we could reapply for visas to go to America.

We enrolled Moish in the fifth grade of the Moriah School and made arrangements for him to eat lunch at a restaurant on our street when we were both at work. Having been warned that Israeli drivers have little regard for traffic rules, we guardedly bought him a bicycle that he could ride to school.

I found employment at the Ran Batteries factory in Tel Aviv. They had a contract to service batteries for the Israeli Signal Corps. My job was to teach the soldiers how to maintain the batteries. However, the shipment of 1000 batteries ordered from the United States had not yet arrived. While awaiting its arrival, I had other duties, including helping with the firm's English correspondence. While this position was fine, I soon realized that we could not live on my pay from this job alone.

My working hours at the factory were from 7 a.m. to 4 p.m. To increase our income, I found a part-time job with a company called Lion the Printer, where I worked from 5 p.m. to 10 p.m. My responsibilities included the planning and installation of road signs. Using an ordinance map, I ordered signs that provided directions and distances to major locations and planned for their installation. My job with Lion the Printer lasted for the duration of the *Mif'al Hash'latim* (Road Signs Project).

The year was 1949. Israel was an emerging state, lacking in both food and foreign currency. The economic situation was at an all time low. This period was called *Tzena*, the Hebrew word for austerity. The government strictly enforced the policy of rationing food, furniture, shoes, and other necessities. While almost anything one could want was available on the "black market," we could not afford the high prices demanded. We had only our small rationed allocations. Food rationing applied to everything except peanuts and oranges, which were freely available. Israelis adapted to austerity as they always have done when encountering a hardship. We adapted as well.

Martha relates:

Apples were a real delicacy – something to be treasured. One day, we went to the harbor in Haifa to say goodbye to a cousin who was returning to America after a visit with the family in Israel. As we stood on the dock, waving goodbye, a sailor tossed an apple from the ship. I caught the prized fruit, which I took home and cut into seven slices. I gave Moish one slice each day as a special treat.

Pinkas continues:

Even with my two salaries, we had difficulty managing. By now, Martha was an accomplished dressmaker. To augment our income, she placed an ad in the local paper, offering her services. Because we did not have a sewing machine, she worked in her clients' homes. Using their materials, she created dresses from sketches they provided or from pictures they cut from magazines. Her services were soon in such demand that clients sought her out, and she no longer needed to advertise.

One of Martha's main clients was the owner of the Sharon Hotel in Herzliah. Martha was provided with lodging in the resort hotel for several days at a time while she made dresses for the hotel owner and her daughter. The pay was good, and Martha liked the work.

As difficult as these times were, we still managed to make time for recreation. As the expression goes, all work and no play makes for a dull life. Moish had become interested in photography and obtained the equipment needed to develop and print his photographs. Of course, he needed a darkroom, which was a problem in a one-room apartment. So, on Thursday evenings, he turned our room into his darkroom, and Martha and I could go to bed early or go out to the movies. We chose the latter, and Thursdays became our movie night.

On Fridays in the summer, when *Shabbat* (Sabbath) started late in the day, Moish and I would take our bicycles to the Galei-Gil swimming pool in Ramat Gan, where we enjoyed ourselves for a few hours. I took the opportunity to teach him how to swim. He was a quick learner.

In the summer, we sent Moish to Camp *Kfar Batya*, which was operated by Amit. It was nothing like his summer camp experience in England, where we could not afford to visit him, not even when he was ill. Camp *Kfar Batya* was very different. Everything was clean and new, and the cost was reasonable. For as long as we stayed in Israel, Moish spent each summer there as an assistant to the swimming instructor.

When my part-time job with Lion the Printer came to an end, I looked for another position to improve our economic condition. I found employment with Ohmotherm, a company that manufactured electric stoves and hotplates. They also had a department that specialized in converting imported electric appliances from 110 volts to 220 volts, which is the operating current in Israel. I headed this busy department until we immigrated to America.

We had not applied for naturalization in Israel because we did not intend to make our permanent home there. Nevertheless, I was recruited and served for a time in the *Miluim*, the Israeli Army Reserve. I was trained and classified as a *kavan* (sniper) because I was skillful enough with targets and clay pigeons. How well I would have performed with human targets is a matter I did not want to contemplate.

In an attempt to improve our living conditions, we applied for a residence in a new *shikun* (housing project) that was under construction in Ramat Gan Bet. We contracted for a two-room cottage and put down a deposit. When the project was nearing completion, we were called to the office, where they showed us a map from which we were to choose our location. I looked at the map and realized that all the cottages had only one room. When I objected to this, the manager asked us how many children were in our family. I told him the size of the family was not relevant, as we had contracted for a two-room cottage and would accept nothing else. He countered by saying that we could add an extra room later. I was furious and asked for our money back since I was not in the construction business and had no intention of building another room. They returned the deposit without too much of an argument.

On the way home, we passed by a small house where we stopped to ask directions. I was also curious about the nameplate on the door, which read "Heinz Isaak." I told the owner our story and added that, at the moment, I felt like going back to England. He said he would go to England or America tomorrow if he could. I understood.

Our unfortunate real estate experience was one of the last straws. We decided to reactivate our visa applications for the United States. With so much going on, we had put that decision on the back burner.

We contacted the American Consulate. Since new x-rays of my lungs were needed to determine that the old calcifications had not changed, we were given a date for a physical examination. I showed the doctor the x-rays that had been taken years earlier in London, and he took new x-rays for comparison. He took a gastric biopsy as well, a procedure I found extremely difficult. The same procedures were repeated three months later. To my delight, the doctor concluded that, as far as my medical condition was concerned, he could give us the go-ahead to reapply for our immigration visas to the United States. We were very happy with this good news and looked forward to joining family members who had already immigrated to America.

Martha's sister Eva, who had lived with her husband and children in Portugal during the war, was the first to immigrate and settle in upper Manhattan. Jenny and *Mutti*, whose journey had taken them from Portugal to Jamaica and Cuba, where Jenny met her husband Arthur, had immigrated to America and were living nearby. Leslie and Benno were there as well.

Much of my surviving family had also immigrated to the United States. Hilda, Max, and Miriam had immigrated first, while we were living in England. Bernhard had emigrated from Israel and Jonas from London. Even my younger brother, Josi, had immigrated to the United States after selling his import business in Calcutta, India. They were all living in New York, where we hoped to settle in the near future.

Martha narrates:

Since Moish turned 13 while we were waiting for our applications to immigrate to the United States to be approved, his bar mitzvah was in Israel. We were very happy that my mother came to celebrate with us. During her stay, she lived in a rented room nearby.

Despite all the shortages in Israel, I had managed to save a small stockpile of rations. We added this to the extra rations the government allocated for a bar mitzvah and, with the addition of some goodies sent to us by friends in Belgium, managed to put together a delicious menu for the *kiddush* in *shul*.

The crowning touch of the meal was the large dessert cake my mother had baked using the only available egg — another miracle! Moish indicated that he would love to have an accordion as a bar mitzvah gift. All we could give him was a promise, which we fulfilled within weeks of our arrival in New York.

Pinkas narrates:

The year was 1953. The day finally came when we were called to the United States Consulate for a determination on our visa application. At this point, it was simply a formality. With all of our documents already submitted and my good medical reports, our visas had been pre-approved. We presented our stateless travel documents and Moish's British passport. With three imprints of a rubber stamp, we were cleared for admission to the United States.

When we departed Israel, the exchange rate of seven Israeli *lirot* for one United States dollar was very disappointing. Although we had been able to sell some of our assets and had even managed to recoup some of the "key money" invested in our apartment, we were unable to raise enough for the trip and have money left over for start up expenses when we arrived in New York. Since our travel expenses had to be paid in dollars, we borrowed $500 from a friend, with a promise to repay it as soon as possible after arriving in America. Despite our precarious financial situation, we were excited to be taking this next step in our journey.

Our travel itinerary began with sailing aboard the S.S. Negbah from Haifa to Marseilles in the south of France. From there, we traveled by train across France to Paris. We stayed for one night at the Charing Cross Hotel, a French hotel with a British name, near the train station. It was a cold day. We sat at a sidewalk café, and I ordered a *café au lait*. Alas, instead of the hot coffee I was looking forward to, I was served ice coffee. I suppose either my French was wrong or my accent wasn't right. From there, we took a ferry-train that brought us across the Channel to England.

We arrived in London the day before the coronation of Queen Elizabeth II and stayed for two nights at the home of Martha's sister Sophie and her husband Louis. The following day, we gathered in the living room with the entire family to watch the grand coronation proceedings on television. The next morning, we took the train to Southampton, where we boarded the S.S. Queen Elizabeth and set sail for New York.

We looked forward with great excitement to our future lives in America and saw no clouds on the horizon. Surely we might encounter some difficulties, but, by now, overcoming difficulties was our "middle name." In the meantime, we enjoyed the experience of an ocean voyage on the majestic ship that was taking us to our new home. As we neared the harbor and passed the Statue of Liberty, we read "The New Colossus" by Emma Lazarus from the brochures distributed on board.

We accepted its message as our personal invitation.

OUR STORY: MARTHA & PINKAS ISAAK

CHAPTER NINE
New York

Pinkas narrates:

We were cleared for immigration without any difficulties. As the shipped docked, we lined up on deck along with the other passengers. Everyone was pressed against the railing, searching for familiar faces. We were happy and excited to see Jenny, Arthur, and Leslie, who had come to meet the ship. We had not seen Leslie since his departure for America, while we were still in England. We had not seen Jenny since we fled Germany in December 1938!

Much had happened during the 15 years since *Mutti* and Martha's younger siblings bid us farewell at the train station in Berlin. Jenny's journey had taken her to Cuba, where she and Arthur met and were married. By now, they were the parents of two little boys, Sammy and David. We had heard much about Arthur, and all of our good expectations were confirmed. Jenny's family met our Moish for the first time. It was a very happy reunion.

It took some time to clear our belongings, especially the very large shipping trunk that Arthur and Leslie managed to hoist onto the roof of their car. Finally, we were off. Driving along the elevated West Side Highway was fascinating. The roadway seemed enormous. This was America! We arrived at Jenny's apartment on 181st Street, where a scrumptious dinner awaited us. By now, we were exhausted.

After dinner, we went to our temporary quarters, an apartment that Jenny had rented for a month from a family that was away for the summer. It was an ordinary two-bedroom apartment but seemed very luxurious and enormous compared to our accommodations in Tel Aviv. It certainly served our immediate needs.

That night, we literally collapsed into our beds. I'm sure we dreamed about America, where all the streets are paved with gold.

The next morning, we began to settle into our new lives. As soon as we had put away our belongings, we went shopping for provisions at stores that had been pointed out to us the night before. We were amazed by the abundance of groceries and fruits and pleasantly surprised by the prices, which were low compared to prices in Israel and England. Our plan was to live according to the modest Israeli standards to which we had become accustomed and put aside all the extra income we hoped to earn. Of course, things did not work out quite that way.

Those first days in America were busy. Enrolling Moish in school was a priority. Signs for Yeshiva University were posted all around, and everyone recommended the school. The Yeshiva University High School, Talmudical Academy, was closed for the summer, but the office was open. We went there to apply for admission.

After an interview with the principal and the Dean of Admissions, Moish was accepted to begin high school in September. They examined his report card from the Moriah School in Tel Aviv and placed him in the appropriate class. We were relieved that he was not required to repeat a year, a possibility we thought might be necessary. They also granted him a full scholarship, which, in our fragile financial circumstances, was greatly appreciated.

Now it was time to redeem our bar mitzvah promise to Moish. We looked around for an accordion, which, in America, the land of plenty, we found easily. We even arranged for music lessons. Moish was a quick learner. Within a few weeks, he was quite adept at it. A "natural" as they say. Not long afterward, he teamed up with two of his friends in the neighborhood to form a band that was hired to play at parties and small events.

Acquiring Social Security cards was an important task, as they were required to secure employment. Martha was the first to find a job. Her duties consisted of sewing snaps and buttons on dresses. The pay was $50 a week. The work was monotonous, but, like everything else she does, Martha excelled at it. Within a few days, the manager offered to make her a foreman with an increase in salary to $55 weekly. Since the work was sectional and did not allow Martha to apply her talents to create a full garment, she decided to look for a different job.

Martha narrates:

I soon found employment with a dress studio that specialized in making sample dresses and patterns, which were sold to small manufacturers that did not maintain their own design department. Unfortunately, I was unfamiliar with the ways of American workmanship, especially mass production, and was fired from this job.

My cousin Berthel, a dress designer who had emigrated from London a year earlier, was working as a designer in New York. She was able to engage me as a sample maker and was very helpful in showing me the intricacies of American mass production. For example, I learned how different it is to make a pattern in preparation for placing 100 zippers in 100 dresses than it is to sew a single zipper in each of 100 dresses when that step is reached. I have Berthel to thank for introducing me to the production end of the garment trade in New York. My newfound knowledge prepared me for success in each of the positions that followed.

After a few months, I left this job to work as a sample maker at Fairfrox, a dress company where I remained for several years. When I was hired, I worked directly under the partner. He created patterns for dresses based on designs featured at upscale department stores.

Since I was a fast worker and completed my tasks quickly, I often had time to observe as he created a pattern. One day, I told him that I would like to make a dress pattern. While he had his doubts, he agreed to let me try. The pattern was a success, and the resulting dress fit perfectly. Eureka!

From that day on, much of my time was spent making patterns. I requested an increase in salary in line with the work I was doing, but the company refused. I decided to seek employment elsewhere.

After several different jobs and numerous trials and tribulations, Leslie Fay, a leading company in the ladies' garment industry, hired me as a pattern maker. At the time, the company's seven pattern makers were all men. At first, they resented my presence but soon began to appreciate my work. They told me that, although my work was good, I was working much too quickly, which made them look slow by comparison. They were quite unhappy about that and advised me to slow down. But overall, our relationship was good.

To the best of my knowledge, I was the first female pattern maker employed in the garment trade in New York. Although pattern makers were not unionized, they had managed to keep women out of their ranks until I was hired in that position. So, in a way, I was a trailblazer.

I had worked at Leslie Fay for a few years when Fairfrox, my former employer, asked me to return. Because of the experience I had gained, they employed me as a full-fledged pattern maker at a salary commensurate with the position.

I have an interesting memory of those years. While she was in Cuba, my younger sister Jenny had earned a good living as a diamond cutter. With her salary, she supported herself and *Mutti*. After Arthur and Jenny immigrated to America and started a family, she devoted herself to caring for their young sons. Sadly, Arthur died prematurely, and Jenny's circumstances changed. She had no income and had to look for employment. Pinkas and I knew that Jenny was artistically gifted and a quick learner, so we thought it might be a good idea to introduce her to the garment trade.

At that time, I was still at Fairfrox. My boss allowed me to take some cut dresses home so Jenny could practice. After work, I showed her how to go about assembling a dress. If she experienced difficulty during the day, Jenny would phone me at work, and I would explain how to continue.

I was both amazed and proud to see how quickly Jenny picked up the "tricks of the trade." After a good while, she felt confident enough to apply for work as an assistant designer, cutting dress patterns and stitching them together. She never wanted to be a sample maker in a factory but preferred to work with a designer. After working at several jobs, Jenny teamed up with Robert Macintosh, a top-notch dress designer with whom she stayed for many years.

As for me, I stayed with Fairfrox for nine years, until the partners decided to retire and the firm went out of business. I did not look for another job. It was time for me to retire as well and devote myself to looking after my aged mother. Her husband had passed away, and we were lucky to find an apartment for her nearby. By that time, we were living in Queens, New York. Having *Mutti* close to us enabled me to provide companionship and take care of her needs.

Our beautiful granddaughters, Sharon and Susan, were born while we were living in Queens. It was a highlight for us to be part of their lives as they grew into accomplished young women. Fortunately, they lived near enough to make this possible.

Pinkas narrates:

After arriving in New York, I began to consider the best way to earn a living. For me, the decision was to set up a business for myself rather than seek employment. Leslie and Ben were established in the costume jewelry business, and I was hopeful that they would give me a chance to learn the trade as well.

In retrospect, I realize that it must have been an inconvenient time. Ben had just joined the United States Army, leaving Leslie to run the business alone. At my urgent request, Leslie agreed to let me come in a few days a week to show me the business of costume jewelry soldering. Unfortunately, it did not work out, as Leslie did not have the time. I would need to learn by myself.

I found employment with Blanche Jewelry, a company that specialized in making shoe ornaments, which they sold to department stores. While the owner hired me at minimal pay, the job was an opportunity to learn the trade. While working there, I became friendly with the jewelry buyer for B. Altman, a department store that did business with Blanche Jewelry. With his encouragement, I resolved to take the plunge and begin my own business.

Three months later, I left Blanche Jewelry and rented a small room on 26th Street and 6th Avenue. Martha's cousin Yankel helped me build workbenches with set-ups for two soldering stations and a work table. I obtained all the necessary tools and supplies, and "Phil Isaak – Soldering" was in business!

My first client was Alan Novelty, a company that made military decorations. Completing their orders was very tough work because it required "hard" soldering, which was a difficult and time-consuming process. As I set about looking for other clients, I went for advice to my good friend at the B. Altman department store. He set up an appointment for me with Avo Selvakian and a representative of Nan-Mar Jewelry, a large and very successful costume jewelry firm. I explained my business to them and said, with fingers crossed because I still considered myself a beginner, that I could design and create jewelry. To evaluate my work, Avo gave me three ornaments and asked me to copy them.

By that time, I had two employees. Gennaro was a solderer, and Maxine laid out the work. When I returned the three pieces and the copies I had made to Avo, he found them very acceptable and said he would give me regular work. In preparation, I bought three delivery cases onto which I stenciled my name, telephone number and the word "Soldering." I left one of the cases with Avo.

A few days later, I received a call from Avo. He had filled the case with sample brooches and the rhinestones that were to be attached to the copies he wanted me to make. I picked up the full case and left an

"Phil Isaak – Soldering" 1960

Photograph in the collection of
The Museum of Jewish Heritage – A Living Memorial to the Holocaust, New York, NY.
Gift of Beth Gerson and M. David Isaak.

empty case to be filled with future work. This became a regular routine. I would return a case full of the pieces I had completed, and he would give me a case filled with new work.

My customers included the famous designer Arnold Scaasi, for whom I made a line of earrings and necklaces that he had sketched.

Actually, I felt that working with Scaasi might be beyond my experience and abilities and was somewhat awed dealing with him in his *haute couture* surroundings. When I told him this, he smiled encouragingly. He said that my work was excellent and he was eager to have me continue manufacturing the line for him. To make me feel less intimidated, I suppose, he also told me that his name was really Arnold Isaacs (Scaasi spelled backwards).

The November 16, 1959, issue of LIFE Magazine featured Scaasi and his work. You can imagine my shock and surprise when I saw that the model on the cover was wearing the jewelry I had made! Although my name was not mentioned, I was very proud.

On the other hand, be it known that I also made tiaras, earrings and certain dangling ornaments for a special group of dancers at Minsky's Burlesque Theater in Newark, New Jersey. My name was not credited there either.

Sometimes we make decisions that lead to unfavorable outcomes. Deutsch Brothers was a customer for whom I made a small line of hat ornaments. While working with Deutsch Brothers, I met a man who was about to form a company that would design and create items to be used by department stores in their window displays. He suggested that I join him, with the understanding that a partnership would be arranged after three months. I agreed, moved my equipment to the new location, and started working at a salary of $250 a week. Three months later, I raised the issue of the partnership we had discussed. Instead of a partnership, I was offered a $50 raise. I decided to leave.

New opportunities soon emerged. The owner of the Kristall Hat Company, a customer of Deutsch Brothers, was ready to retire. I purchased his business. He agreed to stay on with me for a few months as an employee to teach me the business.

At about that time, Martha's sister Jenny met and married Izzy. He was the manager of a ladies' coat factory. Izzy and I soon became good friends. I felt that his manufacturing experience would be of benefit to the new business and suggested that he come in with me. After some hesitation, he decided to do so. With that, NY–UNI–CAP was born.

Soon after, I acquired another business, a ladies' millinery manufacturing company called Zimmerman Brothers. My company letterhead read –

CRISTAL HAT COMPANY, C. L. K. HEADWEAR

Divisions of NY–UNI–CAP INC.

656 Broadway, New York, NY 10012

We now had 25 salaried workers and the business was thriving. I introduced a new and very successful item to the market: earmuffs! I purchased the metal goods from Ewen Brothers in New York, and the plastic parts were manufactured to my specifications in Taiwan. Earmuffs of every shape and composition (fur, fake fur, and cloth) were packaged in boxes of twelve and sold to department stores. One of our biggest customers was K-Mart.

By that time, Martha had stopped working in the garment trade and came in to help with the packaging. We had a glorious time working together. I must mention here that all of my business pursuits would not have been possible without Martha's moral and financial support, which helped to tide us over during the lean periods.

With the purchase of Zimmerman Brothers, our factory had become too small. I decided to move across the street to a building that had been designed originally for individual offices. To convert it into a large factory space, I rented an entire floor and had the partitions removed. But, as always, things change. Our downtown neighborhood was becoming gentrified, and the landlord decided to create luxury apartments in our building. He raised our rent astronomically, which forced us to move out.

I was now 65 years old. A move of our operations at this time would have cost much more than I was willing to spend, so I decided it was time to sell the businesses. I split the operation in two and sold the larger part to Mr. Elias of W & M Headwear and the smaller part, the millinery business, to a another buyer.

Both buyers wanted me to come in with them. I agreed to divide my time between the two parties for a transitional period of three months. After the three months had passed, I agreed to work full-time with W & M Headwear for another six months. As it turned out, this also changed, and I remained with W & M Headwear for almost six years. Throughout this time, Izzy stayed with me and also worked with the company.

Gentrification soon caught up with W & M Headwear, and they were also forced to move when their rent skyrocketed. Small manufacturers were either moving to New Jersey or closing up shop altogether. New York City, realizing the loss of many small manufacturing businesses, stepped in to salvage the situation. They came up with a plan to financially help factories that relocated within the City's five boroughs.

Because Mr. Elias lived in Brooklyn, he preferred to move the factory there. We found suitable space in the Bush Terminal near Red Hook. I then negotiated for financial assistance from the City and helped the company move to their new location. For about two years, I commuted to Brooklyn daily to help them with their operations.

At home, Martha was urging me to begin taking it easy. As a start, we rented an apartment for the winter in Triton Towers on 28th Street in Miami Beach, Florida. Our building was located practically on the beach and had a glorious view of the ocean. We rented that apartment again for the following two winter seasons. One winter, Martha's sister Sophie visited from England and rented an apartment in the same complex.

At the end of our third winter in Miami Beach, we decided to make Florida our permanent home. We purchased a condominium in Winston Towers, which is located north of Miami Beach in Sunny Isles Beach, Florida.

In preparation for our move, I told Mr. Elias that I would be leaving. He and I separated on the best and friendliest of terms. Martha and I sold our co-op apartment in Kew Gardens, Queens, with its furnishings intact. We took leave of our family and friends at a wonderful farewell party given by Moish and embarked on this new chapter of our lives.

OUR STORY: MARTHA & PINKAS ISAAK

Afterword

With great excitement, Martha and Pinkas drove down to Sunny Isles Beach, Florida. Their new home had a terrace overlooking the pool and space for Martha's sewing machine. Now fully retired, they enjoyed peaceful days in the tropical climate of southern Florida. Martha relished her daily swims and power walks along the beach, only a block away. Pinkas quickly became a driving force at the synagogue across the street.

These were idyllic years. Life settled into a happy routine, interspersed with visits from family and friends living close by and far away. Family celebrations at home and abroad continued to be a source of great joy, as they had been in Germany so long ago.

For nearly sixty years, Martha and Pinkas rarely spoke of their lives in Germany during the rise of Hitler and the Nazi Party or of family members lost during the Holocaust. It was during a visit to the Museum of Jewish Heritage—A Living Memorial to the Holocaust that Martha stopped in front of an exhibit entitled "Kristallnacht" and murmured, "I remember that night." The look on her face spoke volumes.

During the years that followed, Martha and Pinkas recorded their memories. In 2011, we published a family edition of *Our Story: Martha & Pinkas Isaak* on their behalf. Like the current edition, it recounts Martha and Pinkas' memories in the context of time and place, from childhood through their 65th wedding anniversary. The Revised Edition includes additional details about historical events and the fate of family members lost during the Holocaust.

A companion book entitled *Missing Pieces: A Family Story Retold* (Isaak & Gerson, 2020) expands the family narrative in an historical

OUR STORY: MARTHA & PINKAS ISAAK

context, from 1935 through 1943. It is based on recently discovered correspondence written by family members who survived and others who perished.

Martha and Pinkas left us with a story of history and humanity in equal measure. From the beginning, they demonstrated the resilience, tenacity, and courage to rebuild while holding fast to the traditions and values that had sustained their parents and grandparents. From them, we have learned the importance of family, faith, fortitude, and tradition.

Their story reminds us as well to recognize those who have the courage and conviction to step forward, to do what is right despite risk or inconvenience. We are reminded again and again of the important roles played by the Briskys, the Ascheims, the travel agent in Berlin, and the Consul in Milan.

David (Moish) was born in Wales, less than a year after Martha and Pinkas fled Germany. He recalls nights spent in the Underground, emerging with his parents in the morning and looking to see if their building was still standing. He was 5-years-old on V-E Day, May 8, 1945. He recalls,

"I remember my parents taking me to Trafalgar Square, where thousands of people had gathered. It was nighttime and very dark—just another blackout it seemed. Then my father lifted me up, onto his shoulders. All of a sudden, like an explosion, all the lights in the world came on. Sitting there, high on my perch under the gigantic neon BOVRIL sign, listening to the crowd roar, I knew something wonderful had happened. A new world had just opened up to us."

AFTERWORD

May we always stand on the shoulders of those who have come before us, finding inspiration, guidance and meaning in their lives, legacy, and the stories they have shared.

BG

New York, NY

December 2020

Beth Gerson and M. David Isaak

The editors are gallery educators at the Museum of Jewish Heritage – A Living Memorial to the Holocaust, in New York, NY. M. David Isaak is the son of Pinkas and Martha Isaak. Related publications include *Missing Pieces – A Family Story Retold*, GERISA INC, 2020.

https://www.gerisabooks.org

OUR STORY: MARTHA & PINKAS ISAAK

www.ingramcontent.com/pod-product-compliance
Lightning Source LLC
Chambersburg PA
CBHW071023080526
44587CB00015B/2473